FADE

ONCE UPON A TIME...

JACOB TSUNDA SALIHU.

Independently published

ISBN: 9798328098625

DEDICATION

I want to dedicate this book to you.

APPRECIATION

I appreciate God, myself, my family and friends for the success of this project.

Contents

POEMS BY OTHER POETS

EPISTOLARY

MY DOVE

I heard about a dove,

She comes in the morning with food in her mouth,

She fly's through the wind with peace in her arms,

Calmness and love she brings,

Smiles and hope she presents.

I heard about a dove,

Her colour is not white as snow,

She has dark spots and she is not perfect,

She is noble and is trying her best,

She is an icon of peace and serves no trouble.

I heard about a dove,

She is beautiful among the birds,

She is free but not careless,

She is lovable and blooms with sovereignty,

She is gentle and weird with charity

She is simple and meek to honesty.

I heard about a dove,

She doesn't sing like other birds,

She is a melody of the heart,

A letter of love not fully expressed,

A potential of joy abundance not fully tapped,

A reservoir of patience by the still water,

An Ocean of blessing with great importance,

A fortress of positivity and character.

I found the dove,

It was not told me all about her beauty,

Her generosity was underestimated,

I was not told enough and I understand,

Nothing can do justice to her personality.

Nothing can express her specialty.

I found the dove,

She flew to my window,

I didn't cage her but she stayed,

I see her daily and I'm glad,

I hear her melody and I'm blessed,

She said she is mine and I weep from happiness pool,

My dove is you.

GOD ABEG

My God listen to me,

I've called on your name,

Don't leave me hanging,

My father,

Help me out,

I've called on you as you asked me to but you seem soo quiet.

I'm almost swallowed up, don't ignore me,

Don't let the storm toss away my faith,

Don't let my distress doubt the genuine-ty of your love,

Don't let my pain lead me back to the arms of iniquity,

Don't let my shame put a smile on the face of my adversary.

You know about my agony,

You can wipe out my distress; why so quiet?

You know about my burden,

You can lift up my yoke, why watch me suffer?

You know about my mid-night tears secret,

You can wipe away my tears, why let me cry?

Your word is true and I stand on it,

Why then do I shake?

You are my father,

Don't make the world see me as an orphan.

You are my God,

Don't let me admire those who go after idols..

You hear my cry soo loud,

Don't make my adversary hear it too and see my tears.

I love and trusted you while I was a child,

Don't make me believe that I was just childish.

God abeg. ....

GOOD OLD NIGERIAN DAYS

In the old times of Nigeria, before now,

When memories were treasured, you would allow,

A journey down a nostalgic lane,

Where laughter and joy were our soul's main.

On Thursday eve, at eight o'clock,

NTA's Super Story took its spot,

After the news at seven unfolded,

Stories of heroes and tales untold.

Lured by the screen's captivating grip,

We gathered around, an enchanted trip.

Little children played football on the street,

With bare feet and hearts full of beat,

The hero, the one who dared to race,

To retrieve the ball from a neighbor's space.

Unified by the game, young and old,

Rejoicing in moments, untold stories told.

A bottle of Coke, a treasure indeed,

Shared among friends in moments freed,
The Coca-Cola cover, a token of pride,
Rotating from hand to hand, side by side.
A sip of sweetness, a taste of delight,
Binding us together, day or night.

Oh, the innocence of young hearts aflame,
When a gentle touch would ignite a flame,
Relishing in the gentle sin of connection,
Embracing love in every affection.
The thrill of a stolen glance's brew,
Transporting hearts to a world anew.

In school, we brought food, one and all,
Sharing joyfully, standing tall,
A potluck feast, a celebration grande,
Feasting together, hand in hand.
Bound by the cuisine of our diverse lands,
We nurtured friendships, forever expanding.

Remember the adverts that charmed our days?
Skye Bank, Indomie noodles, in wondrous ways,

They painted our lives with vivid hues,
Sowing memories we'd never lose.
Iconic jingles that linger still,
Igniting nostalgia, an emotional thrill.

In the old times of Nigeria, before now,
These cherished moments we deeply avow,
Where Super Story brought us delight,
And football united us day and night.
A bottle of Coke sparked laughter and cheer,
While shared meals washed away any fear.
Old adverts, etched in our hearts' core,
Evoking remembrance we forever adore.

Though times may change, memories remain,
Binding us together like an unbreakable chain,
The old times of Nigeria, forever cherished,
In our hearts, their presence never perished.
Let us treasure these moments, old and new,
For they shape the fabric of all we do.
In the history of Nigeria's grand design,
These memories forever intertwine.

IN THE SILENT ROOM

In a room where shadows softly creep,

A writer sits, but finds no sleep.

His pen once danced with stories bright,

Now silent in the quiet night.

Pages blank, like endless snow,

Where once did vivid rivers flow.

His heart, a storm of troubled sea,

Struggles with a silent plea.

Sleep evades his tired eyes,

As moonlight casts its gentle sighs.

His dreams, now ghosts, just slip away,

Lost within the breaking day.

Words once whispered in his ear,

Now cloaked in fog, they disappear.

He seeks to find that spark within,

To light his soul, let life begin.

In darkness deep, he starts to write,

A single word, a flickering light.

Sentence by sentence, a fragile thread,

Begins to weave from heart to head.

Though pain and sorrow weigh him down,

He chips away his thorny crown.

For in his heart, a fire small burns,

Finding strength in its own turns.

Through the night, he pens his strife,

A whispered tale of his own life.

With every tear and every line,

He reclaims his voice, his time.

And as the morning sun ascends,

His heavy heart begins to mend.

For in the silent room, he found,

His voice, once lost, is now unbound.

TRUST

Trust!

I mock your personality,

I shake my head at the amazement of your hypocrisy,

A shameless fellow,

Thy name betraying thy content,

What is seen, far from what it seem,

What is felt far from what is beheld.

Trust!

A betraying mother,

A careers errand to laughter love,

An abattoir of men tagged with rest deceit,

Signboard of a million arrows.

Smoke!

Yes you fade,

Once gone never to return

Trust!

Soo light unshaken by scale,

Soo flexible bent by infant,

Soo large a freezer;

Making the world soo cold.

A cheerful giver of soo much tears,

An arms giver of soo bright a deep pain,

A philanthropist of soo wide plots of depression.

Soo fragile,

A little shake evaporates its glory,

Thin as ice;

Easy to skate.

First built with ease,

Broken to never know the bubblegum taste of cement again.

Trust !

A treasure that ought to upheld when given,

Something better than riches.

THE ENTREPRENEUR

Dreams soo big a night sleep cannot contain it,

Chasing it all day without a slumber but ahead pan,

Walking through with aching bones in darker tunnels,

The needle of the tailor pierces my fingers sweet pain,

Enduring all for a peanut.

Blisters and rolling eyes accompanying the weight of the cement,

Age advancing by labour not years,

Dirty nails and cracking feet.

Wages painted in blood, sweat and dirt,

The wage at the end fills the stomach with soo much satisfaction of nothing,

Large enough that it struggles to get into the piggy.

Dreams soo large but boss tailors slim fit them,

Trouser legs soo large and won't accept even my toes,

Struggles to tear up the worn out local fabric for space,

Melting candle wax every moon time.

Joseph a successful dreamer mocked,

Dreams soo big I want to live in it,

Unfortunately they say sleeping kills it.

MOTHER'S DAY

Mon-DAY,

Tues-DAY,

Wednes-DAY,

Thurs-DAY,

Fri-DAY,

Satur-DAY,

Sun-DAY,

If it has a day in it, it's mother's day.

Conceived in the warmth of unconditional love,

Nursed even when she knows not whom she is to bring forth,

A mother, a clear display of passion unrefined,

A mother a perfect sample of care in human defined.

From her bosom is the first blanket,

From her chest is the first meal medicine,

Feeding her young ones not from the abundance of her full

breast milk;

But from the compassion of her wide heart.

Everyday as long as we wake up and thank God for life;

We ought to stand up and appreciate the root of the life
we've grown to have.

Appreciate the first rent free housing,

Our first free food,

Our first free naked clothing,

All offered in the womb of our super woman.

The fear they nursed while we grow,

Praying that we do not go astray,

We say they are annoying,

Their attitude born out of our safety feared.

Everyday is a day of love,

Everyday is mother's day,

Everyday a mother should be appreciated,

Everyday is mother's day.

Happy Mother's Day.

NICE GIRL

They still ask me questions about you,

I just smile and nod.

You had undeniable lovely sides,

Sides that still tickle me,

You had your moments,

We had our moment.

Memories I had wished to keep evergreen.

My heart frowns,

Pushing its mouth in murmur of the brain signal,

Oh yes! I smile and nod,

With tears in my eyes I smile and nod,

The moments of your evil,

Soo much I wish not to discuss,

I don't want you back and I know I'm sure,

Alright, maybe I'm not soo sure.

I have soo much to say,

I feel soo heavy to say,

Soo much a lot I wish not to discuss with anyone,

Simply because I don't want you to be seen as black.

I don't want to strip you of nice clothing to expose you naked.

A nice girl,

Yes! You are a nice girl.

That's what I say to people who ask.

I then say to myself;

"You are a nice girl I never want to meet again."

ONCE UPON A TIME 2

The journey of 63 years,

An exodus of a people,

Time given will explain the part of the journey to be spoken of.

1st of October 1960.

Oh! What a day!

We danced in pure culture and pride unrefined,

Keeping our differences and excesses aside,

Happy for the newly formed WA-ZO-BIA,

Tongue combination of unity all asking us to come,

A symbol of not just a union of tribes,

But a unity of oneness without sides.

"It was a glorious moment in history" grandpa told me,

Large was the pictures of our heroic patriots hanged,

We were told of their sacrifices,

So with pride he had recite the anthem shouting loud with faith and laughter;

"the labour of our heroes past shall never be in vain"

A new dawn for a great people,

A new redefined area for one people.

Our soldiers match across the street with their kaki soaked in
pride,

Their boots stepping hard on the head of the colo-nization,

Our great soil erected on the beauty of not just flowers but
her people,

The river Niger and Benue connecting with a big Y!

Not asking the question of why we are together,

But screaming aloud the truth of why we should be together.

Our horses stood side by side our great soil,

Hands up in praise to the almighty, showing pride and
prudence,

Our eagle stood with wings wide open in strength and
dignity;

Unity and faith, peace and progress.

It's been 63 years now,

Grandpa tell us,

How has it been soo far?

Grandpa with his aching back stood up,

Pointing at a direction where nothing lies,

Then he said;

"There lived a country", pointing at an empty direction.

"Oh! There lives a nation soo great"

He mourned with tickling tears,

Pointing at a space full of oxygen.

At a place only he could see ...

I TOLD HER EVERYTHING

I told her of the old story,

Now she knows my past.

I told her of the hills and valleys,

I told her of the ship and airplanes,

I told her of the sun and stars,

I told her something special,

I told her the truth with my tongue's integrity,

I told her my depth on my heart's fragility,

I told her everything.

On a rocking chair I sit now and smile,

I remember I told her all that, and now I chuckle.

I told her truths and I'm now held down by her lies,

She gave her ears and attention,

No, not just her ear and attention,

She gave me even more tension,

Yet, I told her everything.

It was a secret,

I couldn't spill it with my mouth,

I held her tongue to mine and I told her everything.

A million promises she whispered with a stain on my lips.

I stand firm in the dock of gentility,

I smiled straight at my stupidity,

Dressed soo fine in my coat of many nonsense,

Her love holding me more firm than my necktie,

Squeezing me more as she testified.

Guilty or not guilty? The judge asked,

Yes! Guilty of telling her everything.

HEAD

Maybe it was all a lie,

Perhaps it never existed.

Listen carefully,

It was all just in your head,

Comeback to self, your imaginations are wild child.

It was never there my dear,

Dig it up, it has no root,

Look carefully, the soil is sandy,

In fact! There was no dream.

Wake up!

Open your eyes to reality,

Once upon a time!

Time... Time ...

There was never a time!

It was all just in your head.

EVERY 90 WAS 20

Adamu!

Oh once upon a time,

A prince charming in his prime,

Fine boy no pimples,

Swag and dimple on flick,

Skin glowing with just water,

His deep voice a rhythm in the ladies eyes,

Oh how he swept them off their feet with a wink.

His six packs more of a sight to behold than his goal,

His broad shoulders wide to provide solace,

Oh how comforting his arms and perfume taste,

His glittering beards, pure and gold.

The joy of every lady,

The bestie of every lover,

The big head of every crush,

The son of every wishing mother.

Oh Joan!

Once upon a time!

Slowly her feet locomotion shakes eyes,

Her shape filled with bullets and bombs,

Moving in a convoy and no mercy ambulance.

Too much she finds difficult to easily command them,

She moves in majesty,

Wagging her hips right and left to the beat of the clock;

Tik tok! Tik tok!

Soo loud are the sirens of her ravishing astonishing elegance,

Blowing in the majesty of her excursion,

A slay queen she sits on her throne,

Her sword at her right hand she social medialy slays,

Glow-ria she is hailed,

She uses an imported tongue; she is foreign,

Back, front, fine, she come sabi cook ...

Normally she be wife material

Hmmmm!

Once upon a time,

A leaf soo fresh to cut now dried,

A flower once glowing in beauty,

Firm in elegance, glory, dignity, beauty and strength.

Hmmmm lets now have a minute of silence,

Let's close our eyes for a second,

Behold the fading beauty.

Fade! Fade!!

Oh! Adamu,

Oh! Joan,

Oh! Once upon a time.

Now they sit on a stool with aid,

Teeth soo fragile to chew Christmas meat,

"Ojuju" the children see them, shout and run.

Their opinions a comic relive,

The package all fallen,

The flawless now wrinkled,

Their beauty now looks wicked,

Their death, a reason for celebration.

What give's meaning to 90 is 20,

What shape's 90 is 20,

What give's 90 satisfaction is 20,

Watch the 20 to be glad at the 90,

Because; every 90 was once 20,

But not every 20 will be 90.

OLD SKOOL LOVE

Let's take this love old skool,

When we were all poets at the touch of love,

The strength of our writings,

The triggers of our ink,

The fragrances of our pages;

Blasting with each word the genueity of our minds and heart,

Not copy & pasted caught fishes on the net.

Let's take this love old skool,

When we scream to see a letter,

Not read and left on a double tick,

When letter not received is worry of safety,

Not agony of suspicion and doubt.

Let's take this love old skool,

When meeting each other meant soo much than yonder,

When we fashion our growing Afro to suite each other in passion,

Not dreads to give ourselves twisted fake compassion.

Let's take this love old skool,

When we hug each other in purity,

Loving each other in totality,

Respecting each other's dignity,

Submitting in love's totality.

Let's take this love old skool,

When the potency of our heart glare's in our action,

Putting in much effort and attention,

Not being restricted by distance and fractions.

Let's take this love old school,

When I say I love you and you feel shy,

Telling me same and I know you are mine,

Not asking you and saying that I pry,

Your shy self an expression of guilt to make me cry.

Let's take this love old skool,

When we both saluted each other,

Respected our bodies, selves and opinions,

We both matter to each other even when there are onions.

Let's take this love old skool,

When the beauty of our romance was in a stroll,

Not defined by ice cream, meat pie and shawarma,

Or prescribed by spree, Lexus and tents.

Let's take this love old skool,

Down to the fountains of young love on the first day,

Our compassion interwoven with care,

When our separation made us fear,

We ache to have each other soo dear.

SIDES

Grew up in the north,

My name is Olumide Olusegun,

Nigeria sent me to serve her in Enugu,

The ladies there are pretty and fair,

My eyes ran to and fro then rested on Chioma,

Paid the bride wealth in sweat and blood.

The church called us one,

God sanctified us as one,

Parents both blessed our union.

Nkenji keke we danced,

In Gargagiya we posed in royalty,

Oruka blessed the rhythm of our union so sweet,

My kids are; Usman, Segun and Chigozie.

The green and white go against the yellow, green and red,

Then you ask me to pick a side.

Are there sides with me?

You put a knife to my throat and ask me to pick a gun,

You weigh my loyalty by taking the life of Kabiru,

(Kabiru's brother once bought me a meal while I starved in school.)

You call me a snake for not cutting the throat of Chibuzor,

(Chibuzor's sister gave me clothes in Enugu while I seek to blend.)

You call me a coward for not castigating Adeleke,

(Adeleke's uncle gave my family a house.)

You tell me to pick a side,

Ask me to pick from Davido and Wizkid;

I love Skelewu and Azonto.

Ask me to pick between Tiwa and Yemi;

I love Eminado and Johnny.

There are no sides,

There are no favorites,

Humanity is supreme.

You tell me Shettima is my enemy,

Simply because he put his head on the floor to pray.

You tell me David is evil,

Simply because he calls 'Jesus'.

You ask me to pick a side from both my brothers,

There are no sides.

MY LAMENTATION

I'm not drunk,

Why then do I feel intoxicated?

I don't smoke,

Why then do my feet feel above the cloud?

I have no cold or fever,

Why then am I shivering?

I need no drug,

What could be my cure?

Who do I run to when everyone is running?

Who do I talk to when everyone is talking?

Who do I speak to when everyone seems deaf?

Who do I cry to when everyone often forgets to care?

My Solace is now my accuser,

Where do I find refugee?

My families are now my tormentors,

Where do I find shed?

My friends are now my mockers,

Where do I find comfort?

The distress in my soul seeks no cooling,

The panic in my heart seeks no shelter,

The weight of my spirit soaked deep in the pool of agony,

My faith, the subject of my defiled fate,

My broken feet soiled in the mud soo slippery.

Where do I go to?

Who do I talk to?

When will I get free?

How will I break free?

The silence of Abba father more than tormenting me,

I had sort you from Genesis,

Don't let me crawl down Exodus to my revelations in this
Lamentation.

Dear God,

Are you there or am I just the one here?

ROYAL CLOWN

Why do I keep doing this to me?

Its seems I enjoy the beauty of the pain now,

More I offer love to the reason of my tears,

Less concern to the giver of my smile.

I remember every hurt,

It's ever green in my memory; every cut,

It's ever revealing in my conscience; every but...

It all lives rent free in my memory; every lost.

You were an idiot;

Yet I saw a prince charming.

I am an angel;

Yet all you see is a bitch.

I wanted us to make love;

You just wanted to fuck.

When I gave you friendship,

You thought I was lonely.

When I gave you relationship,

You thought over you I had no sleep.

When I gave you my heart,

 You thought it was ludo.

When I gave you a kiss,

You thought I had too much gloss and was just sharing.

When I gave you sex,

You called me a horny whore.

When I gave you money,

You thought I had no need for it.

When I gave you support,

You saw me as stupid.

When I gave you respect,

You called me weak.

When I gave you my time,

You thought I was jobless.

When I gave you attention,

You assumed I was just bored.

When I gave you faithfulness,

You thought my DM was empty.

When I gave you everything,

You thought you deserved it.

Yes I find myself in chains,

Thrown you to seek you again,

Gone away from you to return,

Far from you to end in your bed.

I am a dancer,

So I dance.

I am funny,

So I make jokes.

I am a clown,

So I stick to you.

I am a slave,

So I love.

You live in the circus of my golden heart,

You are my guest,

I try to entertain you,

I am your clown,

Your royal clown.

MY SEARCH

It's difficult to find,

I found one but I was not ready,

I saw two but I was too busy,

Now I'm ready,

I found none.

SIMPLE COMPLEXITIES

A compound of tenants with tenacity,

Face me I face you with audacity,

Growth in a compound with reality.

Picked ahead and tossed up high with no assurance,

Lay down two options with no choice alternative,

Patience losing her name virtue fragile to tolerance.

Slowly Faith too loses faith in fate,

Kissed, spanked and moaned by a mighty rod of betrayal,

Crowd of water distress overflow sweeping the moonlight
moments of rest.

Munch it with Netflix a comfort,

Comfort? Bringing everything to the table but her name,

Earpiece bringing calmness to the soul of Peace,

Stagnant and fading, standing and can't go forth.

Sometimes I count myself insane,

Running from good that pursues me to drink from a mirage
lane,

Individuals held in high esteem counted once again,

But all is faded, they bring nothing but pain.

PROTECT ME

Oh lord!

I am on my knees this day to pray

I humble myself with too many to say

You are the door;

You will not shut me out.

You have overcome the world;

My challenges not exclusive.

You are with me till the end of time;

I have never been alone.

There are no demons after me;

They are under my feet.

There is no curses in my family;

I belong to the family of Christ.

I don't carry any curse;

I am the blessed.

I don't carry frustration and hopelessness;

Christ is in me, my hope of glory.

The lord is my shield;

He has helped me.

I don't need to kill my enemies;

I pray for them.

I don't need to pray that they die by fire;

I pray for their salvation.

I am protected from external heat;

The lord is my shepherd.

The enemy outside are scared of me;

Protect me from the enemy within.

Protect me from myself,

Protect me from my flesh,

Protect me from my fears,

Protect me from my bad habits,

Protect me from my character,

Protect me from my unbelief,

Protect me from my lust,

Protect me from my heart,

Protect me from my mind(set),

Protect me from my addiction,

Protect me from my power.

I tried but my strength failed me,

My enforced discipline did not help me,

As you dwell in me, be comfortable,

But defend and protect me from myself.

TRADE

Our relationship was like a trade deal,

I believed in it wholeheartedly.

I invested all my emotional capital

Time, energy, love; hoping for a substantial return.

This wasn't a hasty transaction;

I evaluated the risks, assessed what I had to offer,

And believed in the potential for growth.

My end of the bargain was to be supportive, loving, and always present,

Hoping that in exchange, I'd get the same amount of care, respect, and understanding.

But as time went on, the balance sheets began to show deficits.

The returns were far less than I had anticipated,

The assets of trust and affection were depreciating.

I kept thinking, "Maybe this is just a temporary dip,

A market fluctuation." So, I doubled down.

I gave more, hoping that would stabilize things and perhaps turn the tides.

I was essentially bailing water out of a sinking ship,

Believing it would eventually float.

But the reality hit hard:

No matter how much I invested,

The market would not correct itself.

The emotional dividends I yearned for never came.

My resources were diminishing,

I was left drained, bankrupt of feelings and spirit.

I finally realized that some trades are doomed from the start.

No matter how much you give,

If the other party isn't reciprocating or matching your
commitment,

The trade will fail.

It was a painful lesson in emotional economics,

Showing that love, much like any investment, requires
balance and mutual benefit.

In the end, I had to cut my losses,

I realize my worth, and walk away.

Though it left a scar, I learned that not all investments will
yield positive returns,

And it's vital to recognize when to stop pouring into a losing
trade.

I TRUST YOU

I sure know I could be difficult and sometimes very annoying,

I always remember the aches of my hunting imperfections,

I have in mind daily my inferiority Soo large and complex,

You need not to remind me of my crystal clear nagging,

Clearly aware that I could be such a child most at times.

Not ignorant about the beauty of lady friends you call "bestie",

I have seen the way more adorable women wag their hips in your eyes,

I stand as a witness to your better behaved crush,

Yes! I see the virtual friends with benefit application letters you receive on air,

I heard about how you shredded the heart of many a few ladies.

I see posts on heartbreak daily but I laugh with fear,

I see blooming relationships turn to a union of strangers,

I see plantations of flourishing love turn barren,

I see fountains of love assurance turn desert,

I see promises of the future turn lies.

But ...

You say it's me you love,

I know it's too much a risk to take but I take it,

I put behind everything my head has told me and forge ahead
with you,

I am confident you won't give me reasons to consider doubt,

I believe we won't one day become strange strangers,

Options available but I pick you not minding if I'm right,

Hope I'm not wrong.

A heart is more fragile than a glass I trust you will keep mine
safe.

I trust you won't judge me; you know my past.

I trust you won't hurt me; you know my weakness.

I trust you won't let me down; you know my strength.

I trust you won't break my heart; you own my heart.

I trust we won't fade; we could work out anything.

I trust you.

SCREEN PAPER

On my phone you save my screen,

I chat and touch your face on the keys,

While I search my heart I look at you for a kiss,

Your thought without your presence torments me to miss,

Never get tired of you at any point to even hiss,

You said you are a Miss please be my Mrs,

Your dad's name is awesome but not yours,

Take my name and own it; it's all yours.

On my PC you paper my wall,

I work on it and I click out to see your face,

I look at your smile and it injects my stress with strength,

I see your face and my confusion is trashed with no mess,

I love you; I swear I mean nothing less.

GIFT FOR A WRITER

It's the writer's day,

The day of the world given gift,

What shall we give unto his excellence?

What shall befit his honour?

What shall express our understanding of his texts?

He has written on vanity,

What shall he uphold?

He has written about the Judas kiss,

What shall he trust?

"Give him a car" says the man in black,

He will ride in it and write about its vain.

"Give him a house" says the man in white,

He will live in it but will say he doesn't live for it,

"Prepare him a dish" says the beauty in pink,

He will dine in it and admire the help of the toilets help in its exit

"Give him some designers" says the young man in green,

He will cover his naked body and uncover its lies.

What shall we offer this writer?

What shall he uphold?

What shall he smile to behold?

What shall he pick to adore?

What shall he value and not ignore?

"Offer him a gun" says the wise man,

The gun with bullets of ink,

He holds that in sky's esteem,

He matches with it as a companion to defend himself,

The put it down to attack their defense.

Give him a pen not to fade,

Give him the immortal weapon,

Give him something longer than memories,

Give him something glorious than history,

Gift him something better than good thought,

The shortest pen he shall magnify.

THE BEAUTY OF THE FABRIC

You cut me off?

You did it silently and I see.

You pulled me off?

You did it disrespectfully and I feel.

You cut me off is a win,

You pull me off is answered prayer,

On my knees I spoke to God,

Went hungry in prayer for my needs,

"Grant me permanent and real blessings" I pray,

I knew the implication of those words,

I was prepared for those wars,

I was prepared to loose myself.

You cut me off!

An answer to my prayer,

You pulled me out,

A blessing to my supplication.

It looked gone and faded,

It sound bitter and beaded,

It looked awful and sick,

But that is the beauty of the fabric.

MAMMA

Mamma is not just a name;

Mamma is completely a Blessing

Her smile gifts my day favours

Her smooth voice grace my day with pleasure

Her unique gaze strengthens my day with peace

Her priceless giggle honour's my day with joy...

In Mamma I find solace and comfort,

It doesn't matter if she made mistakes;

I forgive her and she remains my Mamma.

They say a lot about her but forget that she is a super woman.

Mamma's worth is a value no man can afford,

She is a treasure no ordinary miner can reach...

Mamma is precious to me and I love her,

Mamma is special to me and I cherish her,

'No place like home'; her heart is my home.

Mamma may not have it all but she has me all,

Mamma is a queen beyond shallow crowns and thrones,

For she is not a queen because I am a king,

But I am a king because Mamma is my queen...

SUNDAY SERVICE

Gathering of the saints,

Fellowship of believers,

Union of faith,

Heads of mates.

The sound of the prayer Amen!

The preacher stands to speak,

The itchy ears sit to pick,

The mouth affirming strength,

The mind disregarding bends.

The week is blessed with favour!

The preacher proclaim to his fellow sheeps!

Amen! The sound of a thunderous deep.

Raise your hands up to heaven!

Receive with faith for your haven!

Answer loud for your glory!

The loudest gets it the fastest!

Amen! Screams of needs received,

Silence! Feel of touch insecure,

"Abortion is blood on your head" the preacher says,

Bowing heads and urges to leave arouse.

NOT MY FIRST TIME

I stand here in the dock,

Everything seems familiar,

I gaze at the judge cloudy face,

Not soo new,

I've been judged severally by a lady in wig.

Why am I here?

"For trail" I am told,

Yet another trail?

Have I not been tried enough?

I know I stole but my major crime is being a man.

Have been subjected to hand cuffs,

It's all familiar,

I know what it means to have my hands tied down,

All I owned taken away,

I know what it means to be empty for the judge in wig.

Guilty! I am declared,

I'm not surprised,

Judges in wig have sentenced me to frustration.

I am guilty;

Guilty of being a man.

Pushed roughly out of the dock,

Oh! This is soo familiar,

My gender can all relate,

There has always been no love for the boys,

My kind can attest,

They all own no unconditional affection.

Pushed to my prison,

No hopes of visitation till I become my nation's President,

All in the company of innocent victims with crimes of being male,

"Are you new here?" they asked me,

No! This is not my first time.

WHY DID YOU?

The warmth of the summer graced our affection,

We had endless conversations,

All through the hours we spoke,

Still, we had much to say.

The cold breeze of December came,

The frosty lonely street led us to the star,

I remember the smile,

You laughed soo real,

Maybe nothing was funny,

Your laughter gave me an unprecedented joy,

You laughed like glory.

I needed no weed;

You were my highness.

I needed no sleep;

You were my dream.

I needed no light;

You were my sunshine.

I needed no molly;

You were my smile.

I needed no food;

You were my strength.

We stood before the cloud,

It was just you and I,

It felt like it was an army,

It roared in the sky and threatened to explode us,

You kissed me and held my hand firm.

Drizzles came,

You showed your true colour,

I thought you will standby me through it all,

I thought we were an army,

I was just a singular army.

I can't help but ask myself why,

I scream soo loud and I wanted to ask you why,

Why did you do it?

Why did you just leave?

Not even a goodbye.

THE BRIGHT SHADOW OF THE NIGHT

The beauty of the moon's shadow,

The magnificence of the midnight steps,

Flow down the rivers of the moonlight company,

The bright shadows of lovers in each company,

The nice aroma of fries along the side of the black floor.

The whisper of the night rest flavor,

The taste of the midnight savor,

The delectable delicacy of the dark steps,

The soft echo shout of the black misled,

The beauty of thick match of soft disposed.

The night time,

Moment of closure,

Periods of evil exposure,

Season of white explosive mime,

Hour of tears undefined.

The bright shadow of the night,

Served with rest dish,

Appetizer of distress fish,

Brightness profound in its darkness,

Shadow run away screaming in madness.

HOME

They call it a place of comfort,

Feel free and move with ease on what you own,

They say it's the best place to be,

Do all you want my sweet honey Bee,

A building they profess not to be it.

A place you find peaches and love,

I make my noise and no teacher beat me,

Sleeping with both eyes closed assured of nothing but safety,

Argue on differences with my brother,

My opinion I gave freely and don"t even bother,

Oh! My sister flogged me because she was the elder,

I tell my Dad assured of a fair judgment to make me feel better,

Treated on equity bases and respect always present,

I report to my mother because she dispense justice without collecting a present.

9DAYS

Years keep fading by and by but I still remember it,

I recall it like it was a minute ago,

I recall that black gown you wore,

Your perfume after 7 years still has effect in my nostrils,

I recall it all;

That very night when the cloud open up with drizzles of love,

My allergy shrank and melted it the cold.

Oh! What a night to remember,

You stood in the rain with your arms open wide into the weather,

Stood under the shade not filling the space of the weather in those arms,

I thought I would catch cold,

But your wet hug gave me warmth.

Your question "are you still cold" still echoes in my ear,

They setup a furnace and gave me away from the frost.

I thought my allergies was the rain,

Oh! I was wrong,

My allergies was standing in the rain all alone.

I still recall the heated water from your eyes,

Burning my soul soo deep,

My trembling arms holding firm to your tender face,

Only my lips were cold.

My shaky lips I placed on yours to buy some fire,

You lit it up soo fast.

I held you close to myself,

Not too close but very close,

Yet I wanted you more,

You smiled soo beautiful in the dark,

Held my hands and whispered "no".

Soo untrue when I looked down at you and said I would miss you,

I felt the disappointment in your eyes,

Yes! I felt it in your voice when you asked me if that was all,

My heart was heavy and my mouth filled with emotions untold,

I didn't want to say it,

Not because I didn't mean it but because I was scared.

With a trembling heart I whispered "I love you"

You were the first lady I told that to.

you smiled with delight and reechoed "love" 3 times,

I felt the truth in your breathe when you said "I love you too",

I gave you my favorite shirt to bid farewell,

But you were too greedy, you also took my heart,

You asked what you could give me,

I said nothing,

But again you disobeyed and gave me everything,

Everything and nothing at the same time,

You created a vacuum in me and left it empty,

A bottomless pit you stood at the bottom.

You gave me creativity,

I still use your writing skills,

Just within 9 days you did soo much,

You asked what I will do if I return and find you married,

I said nothing but I think I have a better answer now.

You make me take steps forward behind,

The worst steps of my life,

I took just 2 and turned around to find you missing,

You left and I went.

I could feel the excitement in your voice when I called you
the flowing day,

Little did I know that it would be the last.

I have a message for you,

I have a lot to say,

I need to apologize,

I need to say I love you more freely,

This time, I am sure I do.

I toss this to the sea and pray that I get to meet you one more
time.

CONVO

Having a conversation with God,

Are you coming or should I come?

Don't smile,

Don't laugh,

I'm not joking.

It all seems like I'm winning,

The sounds of the gong and trumpet make a sound of victory,

The sign of victory in jail,

Its not what it looks or sounds like,

Anxiety pointing a gun at my guts.

So empty,

Solomon said it all smoke,

Was there any fire in the start?

I'm exhausted,

I'm weary,

Dear God, can you hear me?

I don't want to talk to anyone no more,

Not even the bottles, lawd, or Siri,

Hit me right back.

Sitting at corner left alone to my thought,

Alone but not lonely,

Is life here something I've gained?

Or…

Is it all just lost?

I don't levitate,

I don't read minds,

Don't get shocked when I read through your eyes,

I can relate,

Yes I was there.

Sent from heaven to school earth,

My jet pack rather too heavy,

Giving me some natural artificial hunchback,

I'm just A teen carry soo much more than 18,

Dear God, school is closed,

Come pick your kid.

IN THE MIDDLE

Trapped in the midst of the earth and moon,

Yeah, I caused an eclipse,

Don't get it mixed up I'm not the Sun,

I don't even shine,

But maybe I'm more than the sun.

Maybe I'm some kind of a heavenly body,

Maybe I'm not,

Maybe it's all just in my head,

Maybe I'm knot.

YOU

Staring into Exodus,

Glaring at life soo empty,

Gathering only for a great scatter,

Heaping up daily with the fear of the unassured later,

Vain in style into the ozone.

A color play, life plays with us,

Giving us dark hair only to change it to white,

The once dark navy blue energy turned sky,

The red brilliant roses shrinking to orange at sunset,

Once upon a time evergreen energy now replaced with a
brown stick.

Everything fading,

The good, bad and ugly evaporates to rain down again,

Change an auto compulsory demand not need told,

Very close is its aroma from afar.

Faith an evidence of things not seen,

Notwithstanding, I have this to assure you,

When the black face and head grasses turn white;

I will be next to you on a rocking chair.

When dark navy blue energy turns sky blue;

I will be with you in the sky holding your hands, admiring your beauty as the rainbow.

When your rose beauty shrinks by time to orange;

I will look into your eyes and still see the brilliance of your beauty from all range.

When your evergreen energy dries us to brown stick;

I will still kiss your lips, read to you, sing to you tell you love poetries soo sweet.

Memories fade,

Beauty fade,

Strength fade,

But when all is gone into thin air;

My love for you will only but blossom;

I love you.

WORTH

I know the price,

Soo high without a numbered figure,

Soo low;

I could easily count the figures,

Not confused, just too sure of the price.

Thrown to be taken,

Misplaced to be valued,

Hidden to be appreciated,

Dead to be important,

Rejected to be loved.

What really is my worth?

What is my value if I am me?

What is my worth if I don't pretend to be someone?

What is my value if I decide not to be like everyone?

What is my worth?

Do I need to change locations first to know?

Do I need to change religion first to find out?

Do I need to change friends to see it clear?

Do I need to pretend to perceive it near?

Do I need time to tell me?

Do I need opinions to boost it?

Must I seek votes to behold it?

What is my worth?

First to my maker,

Second to me,

Lastly, to everyone else.

YES I HAVE

I have thrown things to need again;

I have needed things to throw again.

I have tossed a coin and got the third side,

I have characterized myself by uncertain uncertainty,

I have slept with eyes open in fear of my dreams,

I have dreamt of my fears with eyes open,

I have drunken water to increase my thirst,

I have ran forward to meet my past,

I have cried loud to mock my tears,

I have laughed hard to shield my agony,

I have given arms to help my needs,

I have hated more in my bid to love

I have bitten much to chew but my tongue

I have been driven knot and screwed again.

AND IT CAME TO PASS

Everything comes to go.

Life itself came to go.

It came to pass used 400 times in the good book.

If it ever comes then leave the gate open;

Surely it will find it way out.

Nothing is really yours,

It just came to pass.

A HUGE PRICE

It is a small big world,

Somehow we felt positive and sat atop

Connected through water and blood

We waited for God to fill our cup

We were sure we could conquer

'Light at the end of the tunnel' we say

Hoping for everything and the big car

A huge price they say we had to pay

Looking round at our society

Observing where we came from

How shall we escape the affluence of poverty

Answers beyond find in and out of Google chrome

When tomorrow's bread is eaten today,

How can we escape the luxury of hunger

All we have to do in mind is to play

20 friends cant play together for too longer

How shall we then subdue this world?

We ought to focus, pray and watch yonder,

How shall we escape the bad and embrace gold?

A huge price we have to pay not under.

PARADOX

How things turn on themselves,

How events clash on its sword,

How words match on its vocabulary,

How actions are far from its verb.

Nothing seems fair in life,

We don't even ask to be born,

Now we are born,

We don't even want to die.

The fun is always funny when it's not us,

The story is amusing when we are out of the picture,

The tale sound boastful when we are the villain,

The Karma sound evil when it gives us a gift.

The only shoes we fit into is ours,

The only dress we wear is bias,

The only food we eat is bloody,

The only place we live is agony.

The rich says money is vanity,

The rich don't give in fear of poverty,

The poor says money is everything,

The poor relax and make riches look like vanity.

The preacher man makes his request to God,

The worshipers make their submission to the preacher,

All churches are of the kingdom of God,

No church is the kingdom of God.

The bin of the wise,

A fountain for wisdom,

The library of the fool,

An Oasis of deceit.

Life is not fair, its victims declare,

The poor cry, the rich cry,

The poor regret, the rich regret,

Who then is life fair to?

Life in its mercy's horror is fair,

Life in it distributive partiality is good,

Life in its broken pillars of strength is firm.

Life is unfair to everyone,

That makes it fair to everyone.

MOTHER DUCK AND MOTHER HEN

Eggs lay in hidden corner pains,

The duck and the hen,

Fowls of amazing opposite approach attitude.

"Here comes the hawk oh mother hen",

"Stop him!" she screams and jumps,

Opening her wings in protection of her chicks,

Violent in the defense of her broken eggs.

The hawk comes with smiles,

The hawk picks the fleshy chick with pride,

Lunch is set!

The giant bird needs to eat again,

A change of meal is essential,

A balance diet is necessary.

Here comes mother duck,

Quack! Quack! She leads her ducklings,

On a row they move for a stroll,

"Dinner" the big bird rejoices,

Down he moves for a pick,

He takes his time and selects the best,

Mother Duck Quack! Quack!! Facing her front,

Allowing the giant to make his pick,

She is focused on her stroll and makes no shield for defense,

She is focused and won't fight what she can't control,

What can't be stopped must be endured.

Up! The hawk goes away with one,

Still focused and unmoved the mother Duck moves in pride,

Strange! The hawk returns in shock,

Scared of the silent violence at heart planned,

Returning the duckling gently with apology,

Quack! Quack!! Mother Duck moves unmoved forward.

A LEOPARD CANNOT CHANGE ITS SPOTS

It's difficult to think about you without history

It's difficult to trust you without mystery

It's difficult to accept you without suspicion

It's difficult to love you again with all passion

I gave you my heart once and it was all of it

I slew altar sacrifices and gave you all to eat

I gave you my mite, height, light and last bite

I loved you soo much and more with all my might

I gave you a 100 without removing my tithe

You left me drained, empty and depressed

I let you go but my heart you still possessed

Day and night I wept hoping you will return

The more I foolish wait, the more disappointed I return

Finally I took the lane to move on and away

I mourned your departure like you died yesterday.

You appeared a couple of times to disappear

Whenever you call, it was for your needs

When I text you with lack, you slowly again disappear;

You've never changed, you see nothing but your needs.

I am not complaining I am just writing a poem,

Leopards change their spots in only literature, movie and poem,

I know you and just wrote you off in lines and stanzas of my many a poem.

Then you return humbled, true and suddenly with love to pair

You said this time is forever and you wanted me soo dear

But...

It's difficult to think about you without history,

It's difficult to trust you without mystery,

It's difficult to accept you without suspicion,

It's difficult to love you again with all passion.

Yet I was ready and willing to start again soo hot,

Then you proved again that a leopard cannot change his spot.

YOUR SON, MY DAUGHTER

Teach your son discipline;

I'll teach my daughter self-worth.

Teach your son self-control;

I'll teach my daughter modesty.

Teach your son respect;

I'll teach my daughter submission.

Teach your son love;

I'll teach my daughter care.

Teach your son giving;

I'll teach my daughter appreciation.

Teach your son truth;

I'll teach my daughter apology.

Teach your son proper communication;

I'll teach my daughter understanding.

Teach your son contentment;

I'll teach my daughter safety.

Teach your son honesty;

I'll teach my daughter trust.

Teach your son values;

I'll teach my daughter humility.

QUESTION TO THE ANSWER

I was confused and wanted answers,

My mother would change the subject,

My father would tell me to go and study,

I talked to the people who claimed to know it.

I didn't know if what they told me was true or not,

I had no one to confirm it from so I believed.

I liked a boy,

I couldn't tell my mother,

She said girls who liked boys are bad,

She said girls who liked boys would get ruined.

She denied me my emotions,

She made me bad.

She ruined me already,

I felt ashamed,

My emotions for him were intact,

My mind was not.

I thought about putting my fingers in-between his,

I thought his lips tasted different and I wanted a taste,

I asked my friends;

I didn't know that they themselves didn't know,

But they said something;

They whispered strength in my ears.

They invited me to a party,

Chidera said it was what big girls did;

I wanted to be a big girl.

Sandra said is what lively girls do;

I didn"t want to be boring.

Nikki said it is fun;

I wanted to have fun.

Nobody told me much more than what my ear itched for,

I was told to avoid alcohol but was not told why,

I was told that... hmmmm.

I woke up the next morning,

Something has changed,

I couldn't explain but I was not the same,

I tried to wash it all out but it remained,

I looked at my mother,

I expected her to see it.

She looked at me;

I expected her to see it.

She didn't see anything.

Written by Jacob Tsunda Salihu and Precious.

THE WOMAN AND THE LADY

Behind every successful man is a woman,

A lady stands in front of every successful man.

What a man can do, a woman can do better,

What do you expect; she is a wo-MAN.

A lady...

What do you expect; she is a Lay-Dee.

A woman is great favour gain,

A lady is a greed you can never satisfy.

A woman is strength; she is multitudes of words,

A lady is a queen, she has multitudes of follows.

A home without a woman is an empty structure,

A house without a lady is peace.

A woman is a wise ant that gather's to feed her young,

A lady is a termite that feed on the woods of integrity.

A woman is trained in discipline,

A lady follows the trend to Britain.

A woman is culture

A lady is a vulture,

A woman packages for virtue,

A lady packages to be well chewed.

A woman's tears is feared by men and respected in heaven,

A lady's tears is mocked as Karma and is pleasurable to the devil teeth.

A woman believes in God,

A lady believes...

A woman is bold, a doer and a dreamer,

A woman is daring, a believer and an achiever,

A woman cannot be compared to nobody,

A woman cannot be matched with anything imaginable,

A woman is a god!

STORY OF HADIZA

Let me tell you a story of Hadiza

She lives close to me and I know her

Not the biblical concept of 'know'; the literal concept.

She is a hard worker and the street is aware,

She is brilliant and her teachers can testify,

She is a little girl with dreams of leadership,

She is a beautiful girl who doesn't just want to be oga's wife,

She is diligent and loving,

She is trustworthy and thankful,

She is not like other kids; she is special,

She is not as other breeds; she is spectacular.

Oh Hadiza,

How can I say your story without tears?

How can I tell your worth without pain?

How can I narrate your experience without anger?

How can I tell your value without misery?

I left for just 3months,

I left when she told me she was 11,

I called her a big girl and she smiled,

A passionate lovely angel,

She told of how she will one day be the president,

I read her speech before I travelled.

I believed in her as I saw her dreams in her work,

I trusted her aspirations as I saw her determination undiluted.

Baban Hadiza what happened?

Why did you make yourself useful in her fall?

Was it really necessary now?

Hadiza is just 11 for God sake!

What does she know about marriage?

Your friend is 65 years old,

What came over you?

I am not challenging you by morality,

Search your conscience.

Maybe it says nothing about murder,

Murder of tomorrow and next,

Killer of dreams awake.

I MISS YOU

Something was indeed missing

Joy felt far away from my grasp

Restlessness wrapped me with thick romance

Loneliness raped my struggling mind

Sadness made love to my hungry reason

Emptiness filled my weeping soul

Weakness engulfed my dreadful heart

I knew something was missing

I was sure darkness was upon me

I had drank from a river I don't understand

I knew something was wrong

I searched for answers but got more questions

I sort the missing piece but it betrayed me

I mourned myself in peace as I rest

Suddenly it was clear

I laughed as I saw the wall writing

I needed no interpretation

I had miss my lover

I had miss her mind mesmerizing touch

I miss the way my fingers romanced her body

I miss every inch of her moan on my white sheets

I miss the smell of her perfume on my pillow

I miss her

I miss my baby.

CLEAN SLATE

All wiped out ready to write again

Look how clean it is

Karma laughed and nodded

'Aha' she said with a smile holding a file

I'm starting afresh, a clean slate

'Tell that to God' she said and kissed me deeply

It wasn't just a kiss,

She held me down and pushed me against the wall.

Oh yes, I remember how slowly she seduced my memory

Beating me red, white. Black and blue

Its all love on valentine

Tied me with a golden rope and made sure I was hard

My memory echoed before my eyes as she stripped me

I asked for protection at least

But she whispered "To protect what?"

She doesn't use Kayamata

I begged to be intoxicated first but she declined

She wanted my mind intact.

She beat my imagination black and blue and wrapped me soo
good

She could never get tired of riding; I lay submissive

For hours she rode and moaned

Each piece of moan was not noise but reflection

Each stroke she took wasn't shallow but deep enchanting
chain

I wish I could escape but I know I couldn't

I got tired and green but Karma is just a simple dedicated
whore

She wouldn't stop riding, her job she does with pride,
prudence and professionality

She offers no mercy until she delivers what she was pain for.

She places value on every penny I spent.

ANOTHER NIGHT

It's another night,

Not a night to sleep; a night to weep,

Not a night to eat; a night of heat,

Not a night to pray; a night to be a prey.

It's another night,

Listen to the noise of the silence,

Listen the violence of your spirit,

Listen to the torment of your demons.

It's another night,

A scary moment of darkness,

A scary moment of loneliness,

A scary moment of bitter memories.

It's another night,

Cry and scream in your pillow,

Cry and scream like no tomorrow,

Cry and scream to find absent peace.

It's another night,

Sleep and dream of mystery await,

Sleep and dream of frustration lies ahead,

Sleep and dream of broken heart and spirit eludes.

It's another night,

Dark hours of depression calls,

Dark hours of sober thought ringing,

Dark hours of empty hope assurance laughs.

I PRAY

Daily I awake hoping it is the day,

A day my helper uses the long awaiting pined location,

The hour moment for history to adjust its shape,

Yes! Today is my day;

I pray.

God when?

Expression of thanks inquiry with bitterness beneath,

Substituting fate with faith,

Hopeful tears I hope to change to attire of joy.

I pray,

I go on my knees and say,

Thank you lord for the price you pay,

Grateful for the life you lay,

Appreciating the emptiness found in everyday.

I pray to the maker,

Remold me oh lord my Baker,

The atmosphere is only but making me weaker,

People around me grow in nothing but faker,

Calls from fam and enemies all just wanting my sneaker.

I pray to you my helper,

Raise me to stand this day for I am only but a leader,

Shine your light on me so I will need no NEPA,

Soar high with me down here is full of grasses with many a viper,

I have nobody, be my papa.

Oh God my provider!

Be my sponsor be my father,

Take me to greater height be my ladder,

Set ablaze the place where my evil billers gather,

Not just the daily bread, I need your shoulder.

I come before you my protector,

The tongue of the anaconda is my to mentor,

I know my enemies; protect me from my friends and mentor,

They poke fingers at me be my guarantor,

They cage me in bondage be my liberator.

I pray,

Let me not fade.

POEMS BY OTHER POETS

MY OBSESSION, MY FEAR

My lover who turn out to be an enemy

My brightest star who turn out to be a dark hole

My peace that turn out to be my greatest trouble

My blessing who turn out to be a curse

You were soo perfect and unique

You treated me like a queen

I sleep every night but my heart is awake

Thoughts of your flawless smile, soft lips, bright eyes, perfect structure and deep voice

I was obsessed with you

But...

I was not the only one

I was not the only queen

I was not your African queen as you sang

You were only an African king with many

Were you even a king?

You covered my eyes with tick faded fabric of love

Filled my jars of joy with the wine of lies

Destroyed my happiness

I thought I was that rib of yours that was missing

I thought I"d found my own

But no... I was wrong

Finally... things change

The love I once had for you is faded

I feel nothing for you anymore

I"ve moved on and found happiness in another place

In another man

You returned with tones of pleading

I accepted you and took you back as a friend

I forgave you

My heart was clean but yours was covered

Your plans soo evil

Your jealousy when you see me with another

You turned my arm of peace to a shake of war

You didn"t want me; you wanted my happiness

You didn"t return to be a friend; you came to destroy

I lost my feel for safety

I"m living hell on earth

Your jealousy fills my large heart with fear

What will you do next?

You were my obsession

Now you are my fear

Jeniffer Haruna.

FIELD OF FEARS AND FLOWERS

Do you ever care,

That we who love you are in tears?

Your fate reaped a field of fear.

I heave in memorial every hour,

Your corpse unguarded, resting in power.

Life"s taste turned out sour.

A field of roses, flowers, and thorn,

Joy and pain, memories burn

More vividly, we fear not to ever take turn.

Nyeri Salihu Jacob.

JUST AS YOU ARE

Out of the blues he appeared

He looked exactly like the angel in my dreams

"this must be a dream come true"

He introduced himself as a friend

A brother not a stranger

An ally not an alien

He asked for my time, I gave him a minute

He desired my attention, I lingered and listened

He demanded that I trust him, I was too quick to

He asked for more and I gave him my heart

He told me he loved me, I drowned in the words of lust

Drowned, I sought a grasp of air from the encroachment of his love

I'd sank soo deep that I couldn't see a life outside it

Bound to earth by the words "I"d never break your heart", I loosed to him for he promised to never let me go

I now belong to him

He asked for my body, I gave him my body

He took it and made it his own

He knew me more than I knew

He had me, all of me

Having full control, he used and misused me

His touch erased my conscience and sense of reasoning

I had no brains

I took in, having a portion of him

„I"ll marry you" sounded soo real, it wasn"t a deception

Not until the reality of heartbreak and betrayal dawned on
me

It pulled me out of the rivers of my love

It threw me on the island searching for a life

I went back to my past, but it fled

I cried in pain but I wasn't heard

He had left me …

I was left all alone to suffer the reproach of my missed

I had nothing except for one …

I had a mirror in my room

It was a mirror of life

I went to see how I looked

I looked and saw how miserable I"d become

I didn"t measure up to the standard

I turned to leave but its spectacular reflection yet called out
tome

"I do not condemn you"

It spelt out my wrongs, yet gave me a remedy

It told me that I was loved

It showed me an identity which it referred to as my true
identity

I looked more like intensely and I beheld a man glowing with
purity and mercy

He said tome; "Come just as you are"

Faith Medugu.

<u>#**7**</u>

Everyday feels the same

Like an old picture in its frame

Whose pasts are full of fame

But it's present a weak lame

Each play calls over to the game

And to every rise a staring shame

Hefty burdens tagging same name

Gloomy clouds, shadows of blame

Favor from pain"s dark hollow pit

Glamour from a wretched horror sit

Savor of a gravy pot beneath shallow lit

An amour against reality for sorrows fit

Every start feels like detrimental ends

Because lies reigns where truth pends

Uncomfortably can"t help but pretend:

Like a piece of fruit your flesh it blend

It"s eating you up from the inside and outside

You can"t .help but scream between life and death

Daily weeping on life"s track of deadly side

Feelings of worthlessness kept lively in yourself beneath

Time flies into hunger of death for an end

But the breez sweeps a melody through your door

The noise eco your name clearly; a little attention to lend

"open up! Open up" with the sweetest tone resounding from the floor

So scared to try, fed enough of lies and esctasis

Yet so sure and bold of the reality in the second as the voices arises

"Open-up, open-up" more real than fantasy(s)

But a little careful at making decisions analysis

"come, open up" the door tempts

"tick-tick, it"s time to let go off your pasts" the clock alarmed

But trauma and depression holds you down in hesitation at all attempts

Restlessly in your pool of hurts, ready to fight it unarmed

Lo, the knock on your door sounds louder and more sincere

Awaiting your courage to pickup the fight and accept the dare

Of life"sill-treatment and hurts unfair

Enough of the feelings of the ends my dear

OPEN UP-OPEN UP its hope at the door

JUST OPEN UP FOR A NEW ERRA

Benjamin Samuel

A MORNING

Watching sunrise in the morning

Shall I stand, go struggling

Finding bread from day to evening

Life is tough, can I keep on pushing?

When I"m tired, shall I remain standing?

The bridge to good life, when am I crossing?

Inside of church, shall I stop praying?

If not, will my prayers be answered?

Is it not enough as I really tried hard?

If not,will this end before I"m dead?

Or I will die leaving nothing to my kids

A bad mother, there I"ll be

Shall I steal or kidnap maybe

My hard life might then be shinning

And I"ll wake happy from sleeping

Watching a sunrise in the morning!?

Deborah Denis

HEART CONFESSION OF A BLACK SUMURAI

In waiting"s grip, I learned with care

Patience, hope"s child, must always prepare

My persistence burns like a glowing flame

Feet may ache, but love remains the same

Yasuke, black Samurai, I stand uphill

Courage shinning bright, I yearn to feel

Your love, to fill the holes left by slavery

My Daimyo, alone, I"ll fight bravely

On this hill, my Katana poised to defend

My heart"s confession, until the very end.

Nyeri Salihu Jacob

WHAT IF ...

What if all dwell on land or in water and there are no birds to colour the sky?

What if there are all grasses and no trees to give shade or if there are all trees and no grasses to be grazed?

What if the sun was made to shine from dusk to dawn and the star had no chance to explore its radiance?

What if the waters under heaven had not been gathered and there's no ground to be tilled?

Trust me I can't imagine life without oat and wheat...what I mean to say is "I can"t imagine life without hobnobs"

I wonder what the world would have been like if there are all fair, tall, slim girls or just dark, short, fat guys and i was meant to remain single all my life.

What if we all have pointed noses and big eyes?

Or if we were all fashioned with full eyebrows and there's no need for the makeup artist?

I wonder the need if there's more than a Faith (name) and we all are writers?

Or we all held the microphone to sing?

What if we all are dancers with no sound of applaud

Or preachers with zero congregation to listen?

I wonder how lousy the world would have been if there were no introverts... just all lousy extroverts

What if we all are good and there's no need for Godly advice?

If we all were gifted to speak on Faith and not on hurt

If we all are without weaknesses and our shoulders are left dry with notears?

What if we all are perfect to learn?

What if we all are self-sufficient?

You don't need me and I don't need you.

Trust me; life would have been miserable without our distinct personalities

Life would have been miserable without my mistakes and your corrections

Life would have been incomplete without you and me

Life would have been complete if you'd appreciate your uniqueness

Faith Medugu.

PRIDE

Hi

Stop whatsoever you"re doing, I"m about to introduce myself

See, of the seven deadly, I am the deadliest

Once you"ve met me, you"ve met them all

I"m the devil"s devil

I remember meeting Lucifer

When we shook hands

War broke out

He fell like lightening, changed his name

And we"ve been best of friends ever since.

See, of the seven deadly, I am the deadliest

Number seven to show that I"m perfect

But I"ll confess this slight flaw

I"m myopic; can"t see beyond my nose

But trust that I"mthe devil"s devil

See the devil is your adversary

But me? The lord Himself opposes

Bumped fists with Nebuchadnezzar

And for that got seven years and animal

Gave a warm hug to Herod

And the worms ate him from the inside out

Humpty dumpty sat on the wall

I gave a little push from behind

On the day you try your ways refusing prayer

On the day you feel there is no God

It is me introducing myself

See, of the seven deadly, I am the deadliest

Once you"ve met me, you"ve met the rest

I"m the devil"s devil

Hi, my name is Pride.

Othniel Bulus

EPISTOLARY

<u>**Dear God,**</u>

Severally, I have written to you about my pains and lamentation, I have wept and accused you of being silent when I needed you to speak. I had lost my cool when you were asleep and my boat was sinking and I thought you cared not if I perish, all I wanted was for you to say 'peace be still'. I have cried and gnashed my teeth while I walk on burning coal, broken glasses, scorpions, vipers and snake venoms, yet you said you loved me. A dozen times I have doubted your love, ten thousand times, I have nursed the thought of you being unfaithful. Not because I never had faith but my faith became my mockery. The devil beat me soo much that I doubted if you took any pain and nailed it as you said.

Dear God, I am sorry. I had blamed you when I was the problem. I was sin conscious but I forgot to be grace conscious. I was trouble conscious and my ignorance blinded me to your peace; you were never silent, you kept speaking but I was unwilling to hear you speak yet I thought I was waiting in faith. You were never asleep, you were always working in me, my greed made me see you as a slow God. You were my peace but I forgot to see that, so I searched for solace in material things; I forgot to see you as enough, when you said you loved me. You proved it fully, you were never unfaithful, you've fulfilled you promises; every word you said. The devil beat me up because I accommodated him. Even while you made your abode in me and gave me all the power and glory, I abused it and became a trekking prince. I forgot to see that indeed you took it all and gave me all.

Dear God, I am sorry I described your character by lies, miracle, anger and situations surrounding me. I had feared an angry God even though I always read about His love, I saw you more in the testimony of men and defined you by my daily challenges and circumstances that surround me, but I forgot to see your full personality in Jesus; the living word. I am sorry I tried to understand you logically with my head, I used dealings of men to understand how you relate with men. I denied myself revelation knowledge because I was rooted deep in the institution of falsehood, so the truth of your word sounded like a rebellion in my ears.

It was never you, it was my ignorance. It belittled you in my eyes. I was soo blind to your love that I unconsciously mistook you for a selfish God. I saw you as a business mogul who wanted to use me and not as a father who is eager to bless me. I saw you as a judge who was waiting for me to sin so he could bounce on me with judgment, I forgot to see you as the God of my salvation who gave up himself so that there will be no condemnation against me. I followed you because I didn't want to go to hell, the fear of hell alone was hell, but right now, if you will go down, I am ready to go down with you.

I forgot that what made me a Christian is your Spirit in my clay body. I was trying to be spirit when you wanted me as I am; clay. I was waiting for you to react, I forgot that you only pro-act;You are God.

It is I,

Your Son.

My name is Jacob Tsunda Salihu and I hope you enjoy reading this book as much as I enjoyed writing it.